By Appoint

RANSOMES
LAWN MOWERS.

The "LEO" (ball bearing)

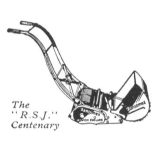

The "R.S.J." Centenary

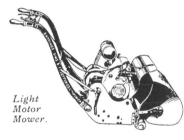

Light Motor Mower.

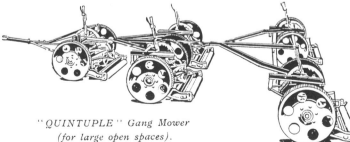

"QUINTUPLE" Gang Mower (for large open spaces).

RANSOMES, SIMS & JEFFERIES, Ltd. have now completed a century's experience in the manufacture of lawn mowers, and at present are able to offer a larger variety of mowing machines than any other firm. During this hundred years Ransomes Lawn Mowers have been sold into all countries of the world, and are in universal use. The reason for this wide popularity is to be found in that Ransomes Lawn Mowers are extremely well built, each machine being a sound engineering job, and also that in the wide range of machines offered there is a machine suitable for any size or type of lawn. There is a mower in Ransomes Range to suit your lawn too, and you may be sure that if you purchase a Ransomes Lawn Mower it will last a lifetime giving good service.

Let us send you our up-to-date catalogue and full particulars.

Ransomes, Sims & Jefferies, Ltd., Orwell Works, Ipswich.
AGRICULTURAL, MECHANICAL, ELECTRICAL AND GENERAL ENGINEERS.
Ask for catalogue of our Ploughs and Agricultural Implements, Steam Thrashing Machinery, etc.

IPSWICH
A PICTORIAL HISTORY

Edwardian view of Dial Lane with the tower of St Lawrence's Church and the corner of the Ancient House beyond. Only those who have stopped for the photographer appear other than as blurs on the photograph.

IPSWICH
A PICTORIAL HISTORY

ROBERT MALSTER

Phillimore

1991

Published by
PHILLIMORE & CO. LTD.
Shopwyke Hall, Chichester, Sussex

ISBN 0 85033 786 0

Printed and bound in Great Britain by
BIDDLES LTD.
Guildford, Surrey

In memory of Paul Richard,
1968-1990

List of Illustrations

Frontispiece: Edwardian view of Dial Lane

Preface and Acknowledgements

One of my earliest visits to Ipswich was when, as a boy of five or six in the late thirties, I travelled with my mother on a special excursion train hauled by Stirling Single No. 1, which had been brought out of retirement in a museum at York to celebrate the centenary of the *Flying Scotsman*. Even at that tender age my interest in history was being encouraged.

I can therefore claim an acquaintance with the town that spans more than fifty years, though it was not until much later that I became a resident of the borough and, encouraged by the late Mr. Harry Wilton and his circle of friends, began to research its history.

The definitive history of Ipswich has yet to be written, and that is a task I must leave to others better qualified than I. It is clearly impossible to provide anything approaching a full history of a town in a book of this size, yet I hope that this pictorial history will awaken many to their heritage and will persuade a few that Ipswich is a town worthy of serious historical study and of better treatment than it has had in the past.

My object has been to select pictures that best tell the story of the town. At the same time I have, wherever possible, chosen those photographs that are not already well known, since more than half a dozen books of old photographs of the town have been published since the appearance of the pioneering *Ipswich Remembered* in 1975.

So many people have assisted with this project that it would be difficult to thank them all individually without offending somebody by omission. Might I therefore thank collectively all those who have helped, both by providing illustrations and by giving encouragement and advice. One who deserves special mention is Mr. Bernard Barrell who, with great generosity, provided me with a copy of Joseph Pennington's map of Ipswich, 1778, and with a copy of John Glyde's *Illustrations of Old Ipswich*. I hope that he approves of the use to which I have put them.

Illustration Acknowledgements

Photographs have been provided by the following, whom I wish to thank for giving permission for their reproduction: Suffolk Record Office, nos. 9, 18-21, 39, 55, 76, 111-13, 115, 119, 127-8, 134; East Anglian Film Archive, nos. 143, 150-1, 153, 168-9, 171-4, 176-7, 181-4, 186; Ransomes, Sims & Jefferies, nos. 83, 85-6, 90; Mrs. Gladys Wilton and Mr. John Wilton, nos. 71, 75, 78-9, 95-6, 132-3, 135, 144, 148-9, 156-9; Mrs. M. R. Leeson, no. 88; Mrs. Margaret Kinsey, nos. 48, 52; Mr. Don Chipperfield, nos. 53, 131, 137; Mr. Bob Markham, nos. 44, 77, 80-2, 104, 170; Mr. Hugh Moffat, no. 154; Mr. Richard Smith, nos. 188-9; Mr. J. A. E. Burrows and Mr. Richard Smith, nos. 122-4; the editor of the *East Anglian Daily Times* nos. 190-1. All other photographs have been provided by the author.

Bibliography

Clegg, Muriel, *Streets and Street Names in Ipswich* (Salient Press, 1984)

Clegg, Muriel, *The Way we Went* (Salient Press, 1989)

Gross, R. L., *Ipswich Corporation Civic Regatta* (Ipswich Corporation)

Gross, R. L., *Ipswich Markets and Fairs* (Ipswich Corporation, 1965)

Gross, R. L., *Justice in Ipswich, 1200-1968* (Ipswich Corporation, 1968)

Glyde, John, *Illustrations of Old Ipswich* (1989)

Glyde, John, *The Moral, Social and Religious Condition of Ipswich* (1850; new edition by S. R. Publishers, 1971)

Grace, D. R., and Phillips, D. C., *Ransomes of Ipswich: A History of the Firm and Guide to its Records* (Institute of Agricultural History, 1975)

Gray, I. E., and Potter, W. E., *Ipswich School, 1400-1950* (W. E. Harrison, 1950)

Hunt, William, *A Descriptive Handbook of Ipswich* (1864)

Lewis, R. Stanley, *Eighty Years of Enterprise: Being the intimate story of the Waterside Works of Ransomes & Rapier Limited* (W. S. Cowell, 1950)

Malster, Robert, *Ipswich Town on the Orwell* (Terence Dalton, 1978)

Markham, R., *Public Transport in Ipswich, 1880-1970* (Ipswich Information Office, 1971)

Markham, R., *100 Years of Public Transport in Ipswich: A Pictorial Survey* (Ipswich Borough Council, 1980)

Morrison, R. K. McD. (ed.), *History of Engineering in Ipswich* (Ipswich Engineering Society, 1974)

Redstone, Vincent B., *The Ancient House or Sparrow House, Ipswich* (W. E. Harrison, 1912)

Wade, Keith, *The Origins of Ipswich* (Suffolk County Council, 1981)

Weaver, Carol and Michael, *Ransomes 1789-1989, 200 Years of Excellence*

Weaver, Carol and Michael, *Ransomes Sims & Jefferies plc* (1989)

Webb, John, *Great Tooley of Ipswich: Portrait of an Early Tudor Merchant* (Suffolk Records Society, 1962)

An Account of the Gifts and Legacies ... in the Town of Ipswich (1747)

The Principal Charters which have been granted to the Corporation of Ipswich (1754)

Ipswich: The Industrial Capital of East Anglia (Ipswich Industrial Development Association, 1932)

Silver Jubilee of the Ipswich Philatelic Society (Ipswich Philatelic Society, 1970)

Through Sixty Years (Ipswich Industrial Co-operative Society, 1928)

East Anglian Daily Times (1874 to date)

Evening Star (1884 to date)

1.   Heavy rain which swelled the River Gipping caused severe flooding in low-lying parts of the town in 1939. One road that suffered was Princes Street, built across the marshes in the 19th century.

Introduction

When the Saxons founded their settlement of Gyppeswyk at the point at which the Orwell was fordable there were no other towns in East Anglia. That was some time in the seventh century, a period when urban life was virtually unknown. Indeed, it is possible that even two hundred years later there were only two or three towns of the size and character of Saxon Ipswich; they were Hamwih, the Saxon Southampton, London and, possibly, York.

Archaeologists working in the town since 1974 have discovered a great deal about the early origins of Ipswich, largely unsuspected by earlier historians who depended on archival sources for their information. Excavating sites that were due to be redeveloped or were to be cut across by new roads, members of the Suffolk Archaeological Unit have been systematically building up a picture of a Saxon settlement which covered no less an area than 50 hectares, some fifty times bigger than the average rural settlement of Saxon times.

Right from the start Ipswich was an industrial town. Many of its Saxon inhabitants were craftsmen, some of them potters producing a distinctive grey ware which was widely distributed throughout East Anglia and also much further afield. Archaeologists have given this the name 'Ipswich ware', for it seems that Ipswich was the only centre producing this form of pottery; indeed, it was the only place in England making wheel-thrown, kiln-fired pottery in the period from the departure of the Romans in the fifth century up to the ninth century.

Finds from the numerous excavations in the town centre indicate that by the ninth century Ipswich was a thriving town producing not only pottery but much else besides. Some of the town's community of craftsmen were engaged in textile production, for spindle whorls used in spinning wool have been unearthed from the Saxon levels, and so have combs made of antler, apparently the products of some of the other craftsmen who lived in the town. There were leather workers, and a bronzesmith whose workshop, complete with crucible and moulds, was unearthed on the site between the Buttermarket and the Old Cattle Market. All these finds point to the industrial nature of Ipswich in this early period.

Royal influence can be seen in this spectacular rise of the Saxon town, for it seems that the town was controlled by the Wuffinga dynasty of East Anglian kings who had their royal palace some twelve miles away at Rendlesham. The most famous of that dynasty, Redwald, is almost certainly commemorated in the ship burial at Sutton Hoo, and the richness of the treasure unearthed from within the ship bears witness to the wide-ranging trade being carried on by members of that royal house.

Their trade was carried on through Ipswich, a trading port of considerable significance then as now. The royal house was importing luxury goods, wine, fine garments, furs and all kinds of other things, but there was also an everyday trade in more mundane goods. Ipswich-made pottery was exported coastwise to other parts of the East Anglian kingdom, to London and Kent and even to the West Country and to Yorkshire, while imports included whetstones and millstones from the middle Rhineland, wine from the same area and pottery from the Low Countries.

2.   The original Town Hall in 1810. It had begun life as St Mildred's Church, almost certainly a Saxon foundation.
St Mildred, who at the time of her death was abbess of a nunnery in Kent, died in about 700 when Ipswich was already
a thriving town under East Anglian royal patronage.

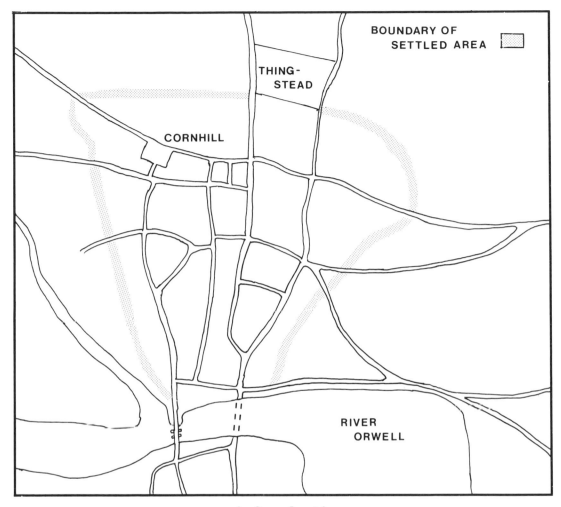

BOUNDARY OF
SETTLED AREA

THING-
STEAD

CORNHILL

RIVER
ORWELL

3   Saxon Ipswich.

These imported goods were landed at the earliest quay, which lay behind the present-day quayside warehouses and maltings in the vicinity of the street we now know as Key Street. Nearby was the site of a summer trading fair that probably had something of the appearance of an agricultural show of some 1,200 years later. The fair attracted merchants from the Continent as well as from other parts of Britain who camped on the land which in later times was covered by the houses of medieval Ipswich.

By the early 10th century the town had its first defences, the entire settlement being surrounded by a large ditch which might well have been dug by East Anglian Danes just before the area was retaken by the English.

The road pattern laid down in Middle Saxon times survived largely unchanged until the 19th century. The main east-west road remains in Carr Street, Tavern Street, the Cornhill and Westgate Street. The main north-south route seems originally to have been Upper and Lower Brook Street, leading to a ford across the river linking up with Whip Street and Wherstead Road, but at some time in the 10th century the building of the first Stoke Bridge, placed upstream of the ford so as not to interfere with shipping using the river, necessitated a change of the route; the old streets remained, but St Peter's Street and St Nicholas Street, connecting the bridge with the Cornhill on the north side, and Bell Lane, linking it with Wherstead Road on the Stoke side of the river, became the principal north-south route.

Ipswich was without doubt an expanding town in the period before the Norman Conquest, for by the mid-11th century it had spread outside the early defences, beyond which were the suburbs of St Matthew's, St George's, St Margaret's and St Helen's. In St Margaret's was the Thingstead, the public meeting place; it survives to this day as St Margaret's Green.

It was a populous town with a mint at the time of the Conquest. Something happened between 1066 and the compilation of Domesday Book, 20 years later, to reduce the population of the town, however, for in that record we read that whereas there had been 538 burgesses before 1066 there were then only 210, and nearly half of them were too poor to pay any taxes apart from a penny poll tax. And no fewer than 328 dwellings had been laid waste. This could be evidence of Norman vengeance following the revolt of Ralph Guader; the Domesday clerk recorded the flight of burgesses from Norwich and remarked that 'those fleeing and the others remaining have been utterly devastated partly because of Earl Ralph's forfeitures ...'.

Another mystery is the site of the castle which the Normans built in Ipswich soon after the Conquest. It is generally supposed to have been in the area once called the Mount,

4. The borough arms as confirmed in 1561.

5. The Common Seal of Ipswich, which dates from 1200.

near the junction of Elm Street with Curriers Lane and Black Horse Lane, formerly called Gaol Lane; roughly where the Civic Centre and the police station are now. It was probably no more than a timber structure atop an earthen motte, the 'mount' of later memory.

The impecunious King John granted Ipswich a charter under which 'Our said Burgesses, by our Common Council of their Town, may choose Two of the more lawful and discreet Men of their Town, and present them to Our Chief Justice, at Our Exchequer, who may well and faithfully keep the Government of the Borough of Ipswich aforesaid; and may not be removed, as long as they behave well in that Bailiffwick, except by the Common Council of the aforesaid Burgesses. We will also, that in the same Borough, Four of the more lawful and discreet Men of the Borough, be chosen by the Common Council, out of the Burgesses aforesaid, to keep the Pleas of the Crown and other Things that appertain to Us, and Our Crown, in the said Borough, and to see that the Governors of that Borough behave justly and lawfully towards the Poor, as well as the Rich.'

Thus was founded, or at least confirmed by the Crown, the system of local government by two bailiffs, a number of portmen and a common council under which the town was regulated until the passing of the Municipal Reform Act of 1835. It was the merchants of the town who had sought the grant of the charter, and it was they who had most to gain from its terms. Already the town and port of Ipswich was thriving as a result of the trading activities of its merchants.

The significance of the port is indicated by the presence on the arms of the borough of three demi-ships and of a complete ship on the borough seal. The seal bears one of the earliest known representations of a ship with a rudder hung on the sternpost instead of the steering oar over the quarter that had served until the late 12th century. The Common Seal was made in 1200, and the original arms are thought to date from only a little later. When Wyllyam Herve, Clarenceux King of Arms, confirmed the ancient arms in 1561 he granted as supporters two seahorses in silver, representing the horses which hauled Neptune's chariot, and a crest which included a demi-lion supporting another ship, thus further emphasising the maritime importance of the town.

Succeeding monarchs confirmed the charter and extended the privileges enjoyed by the citizens of Ipswich. Henry VIII more particularly stressed the maritime nature of the town by specifically confirming the Corporation's jurisdiction over the Orwell and by granting the Corporation Admiralty jurisdiction: 'That the Bailives of the said Town, for the Time Being, shall be Our Admirals, and the Admirals of Our Heirs, for and within the whole Town, Precincts, Suburbs, Water, and Course of Water'.

Notwithstanding Henry's very specific words, there was for very many years opposition from the people of Harwich, who from their position on the south side of Harwich harbour disputed the maritime jurisdiction of the inland town. There could be little dispute over the supremacy of Ipswich in the matter of trade, however, for it was in Ipswich that wealthy merchants who prospered exceedingly on trade with the Biscayan ports, with the Netherlands and with Iceland built their homes and carried on their businesses.

In spite of years of change and decay, slum clearance and redevelopment, some of the houses which these Tudor merchants built in the parish of St Clement's yet remain as a reminder of one of the town's periods of prosperity. At the back of these houses are the warehouses in which the merchants stored the wine, the dried fish and all the other commodities they imported.

The history of the town shows a strange fluctuation between prosperity and stagnation. Daniel Defoe compares the 17th-century scene with a hundred colliers laid up in the Orwell in winter while their masters and crews lay 'snug in their beds at home' with the neglected appearance of the town half a century later when 'it was melancholy to hear that there were now scarce 40 sail of good colliers that belonged to the whole town'.

One of the causes of the decline in the town's fortunes was the silting of the Orwell, which led to the remark attributed by Sir James Thornhill to the dramatist Thomas Killigrew that 'Ipswich had a river without water, streets without names and a town without people'. As the channel deteriorated all but the smallest vessels had to unload into lighters below a point known as Downham Bridge about half a mile below the town's quays; it was not a bridge as we know it today, but probably a timber causeway by which the river could be forded at low tide.

Trade and Commerce

Through fair times and foul Ipswich remained a market town and the centre of an agricultural area that not only provided food for the townspeople but also for export coastwise to London and other places. The name of the square fronting the Town Hall still reminds us of the position of the medieval corn market, and the street name 'Buttermarket' is a reminder of the countrywomen who brought into town their dairy produce. Where now stands the Head Post Office were until 1794 the Shambles, the preserve of the butchers, and behind them was the herb market.

Tradition has it that the Shambles were erected under the direction of Cardinal Wolsey, himself the son of an Ipswich butcher. There had been Shambles in Ipswich in earlier times, and if that tradition be true it would seem that the original earlier building was either substantially rebuilt or perhaps replaced about 1583. More certain is the fact that the Shambles were replaced in 1793-94 by the Rotunda, a building which had a short life; its place was taken in 1812 by the first Corn Exchange.

At the same time that the Rotunda was taken down the Market Cross was also demolished, to the regret of some townspeople at the time and of many more since. It had been built in 1629 to replace the original Cross given to the town about 1510 by Edmund Daundy, who died five years later and was buried in St Lawrence's Church. The Cross had its uses beyond the market business, for it was from its shelter that the annual proclamations of the Sheriffs for the county were read, and it was also used at election times and on other public occasions.

The Cornhill was for very many years used for the sale of cattle on market days. The presence of cattle and horses proved not only inconvenient but positively dangerous to others having business on the Cornhill and in 1812, a year of considerable change in Ipswich, the cattle market was moved to a new site at the top of Silent Street, close to the new provision market which had opened two years earlier. The cattle market remained there until 1856, when a new cattle market was opened on land between Friarsbridge Road and the new road that in later days became known as Princes Street. The surface of what had been a marsh was raised about two feet to provide a firm, dry site for the new market.

The provision market, facing the *Bluecoat Boy* public house across what has been known ever since 1856 as the Old Cattle Market, continued to serve the public more or less satisfactorily following the removal of the cattle market to its new position. G. R. Clarke, the Ipswich historian, tells how 'Saturday is the great market day for all kinds of provisions, and for goods of every description, and the assemblage of vendors from

6.   The Shambles, which stood on Cornhill on the site of the present post office, were 'newly built' in 1583, but there are references in the Corporation records to a building having been erected in 1278. It is possible that the building was merely rebuilt or extensively repaired in 1583.

7.   Joseph Pennington's map of 1778 shows the area of Cornhill as it had been in medieval times, with the Market Cross in the open area in front of the Town Hall and Shambles.

8. The Market Cross, erected in 1628 and pulled down in 1812. The figure of Justice subsequently enjoyed a reincarnation as Ceres on the Corn Exchange, built in 1812.

9. The provision market, photographed by Robert Burrows in the late 1850s.

neighbouring towns and villages is so great that it is not uncommon to see articles, even of haberdashery and millinery, spread out for display upon the ground, the whole exhibiting a scene of bustle and animation, worthy of the observation of strangers'.

Nineteenth-century expansion

The scene in the market was but a reflection of the thriving state of Ipswich as a whole in the 19th century. It was a period of expansion during which Ipswich changed from a provincial market town and decayed seaport to a successful industrial town with a busy dock both importing essential raw materials and exporting the products of the industrial plants which grew up in the dock area. 'Ipswich is a progressive town and the hand of improvement and enterprise has effaced the traces of antiquity, the signs our forefathers left of their existence and their doings, more quickly and more completely than in almost any ancient town you may visit', wrote the author of a mid-century guidebook; 'but while we are glad at the prosperity of the old town, and like the comfort of modern dwellings and wider streets and more imposing buildings, there is among the old inhabitants a strange affection for anything that will recall the features and events of Ipswich in past days.'

That is, no doubt, why William Vick, who set up in business as a photographer in Ipswich in about 1870, found a ready sale for his mounted photographs of the town and of buildings which had already disappeared. He borrowed from the work of his predecessor in business, William Cobb, and of other photographers to provide a series of prints which portrayed a town changing fast and sweeping away its past in the name of progress.

His photographs of the Cornhill, for instance, show the succession of buildings which took their places there during the course of the 19th century. The remains of St Mildred's Church, which had become redundant in medieval times and become the Town Hall, disappeared in a rebuilding of 1818; the porticoed frontage designed by Benjamin Catt that masked the dilapidated medieval building gave way in the 1860s to a new Town Hall 'in the Venetian style' which remained the seat of local government for a century. The Corn Exchange which had taken the place of the Rotunda in 1812 itself gave way to a fine Post Office in 1880-81, when a new Corn Exchange which was also to house the provision market, transferred from its site opposite the *Bluecoat Boy*, was built to the design of Brightwen Binyon behind the Town Hall.

In recent years the Cornhill scene has changed again with the introduction of a town-centre pedestrian precinct and the paving over of what had once been the hub of the town's communications and a road junction busy with traffic. Replaced in its original role by a towering new Civic Centre, the Town Hall has become a meeting place for local organisations, while the Corn Exchange has been converted into a fine cultural centre with exhibition halls, cinema and other facilities.

It was not only in its public buildings that Ipswich changed during the 19th century, for the coming of the railway in 1846 had an impact not only on the town's industrial and commercial prosperity but also on its planning. With the opening in 1860 of a new station at the north end of the tunnel cut through Stoke Hill by Peter Bruff in order to carry the railway on from Ipswich to Bury St Edmunds and Norwich, a new road was constructed across the marshes to link the station with the Cornhill, a timber bridge being constructed to carry the road over the river.

William Hunt tells how at the town end this new road, Princes Street, 'bored through a mass of houses, gardens, streets and lanes diagonally, leaving corners and angles of old

10. The Rotunda, an unpopular building which replaced the old Shambles in 1793-94 and was itself torn down in 1812.

11. Benjamin Catt's rebuilding of the old Town Hall as further modified in 1841. With its demolition in 1867 all traces of the former St Mildred's Church disappeared.

12. The 1812 Corn Exchange as rebuilt in 1849-50 and other buildings on the Cornhill, seen in 1864. The decorations are for the celebrations of Shakespeare's tercentenary.

13. Princes Street was still 'rugged and aboriginal in appearance' when the new railway station opened in 1860, but by the 1890s the town end at least was fully developed. In the middle of the picture can be seen the premises of R. D. & J. B. Fraser, which replaced the offices of the *Ipswich Journal* in 1890. The horse tram lines can be seen in the roadway.

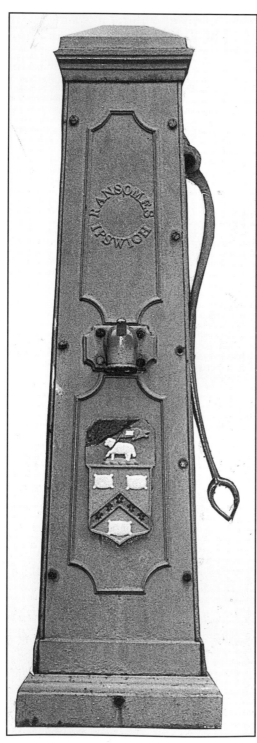

14. A typical early product of the Ransomes foundry is this pump at nearby Hadleigh.

buildings, dead walls with the marks upon them of gable ends dislodged, and bits of lanes running off at curious tangents'. The outer end of the new road across the marshes was at first known as Railway Station Road, but the whole stretch from the junction with Queen Street and the Buttermarket to the station is now Princes Street.

Other roads were also cut through what had once been gardens. Museum Street, constructed in the 1840s, and Arcade Street, which at the beginning formed part of Museum Street, are just two examples. The archway at the junction with Elm Street was cut through the existing buildings when the street was constructed. Only the name of Coyte's Gardens, a backway between Friars Street and Princes Street, remains to remind us of the pleasant lawns and flower-beds among which Dr. Beeston had strolled in the early 18th century and which his successor Dr. William Beeston Coyte had enjoyed at the end of that century.

Industries

The arrival in Ipswich in 1789 of a Norwich ironfounder, Robert Ransome, with a single employee, aroused little interest at the time, but with hindsight we can see that it was a most significant event. Ransome set up an iron foundry in a disused malting in St Margaret's Ditches, today known as Old Foundry Road.

The business that Robert Ransome established towards the end of the 18th century was expanded and developed in the 19th by his sons and grandsons. They took into the business partners who brought new skills to help the firm overcome agricultural depression and take advantage of new opportunities. When the conclusion of the Napoleonic Wars brought an end to a period of agricultural prosperity and reduced many farmers to poverty the firm turned to civil engineering, building a new Stoke Bridge in cast iron in 1818, and with the coming of the Railway Mania it diversified into the production of railway equipment.

When in the mid-19th century opportunities to export agricultural machinery to the colonies and the New World prompted an expansion of this branch of the company's work, the railway department was hived off to a new company, Ransomes & Rapier, and to a new works on the other side of the river. That company made its name by building the first railway in China and later by constructing sluice gear for such projects as the Aswan Dam on the Nile.

In the 1840s Ransomes began producing steam engines, many of which were exported to power the thrashing machines produced in the company's Orwell Works. Another firm to build steam engines in the town was that founded in 1837 by Mr. Walton Turner and two partners; it was to become well known as E. R. & F. Turner, and as such was to play a leading part in the introduction to this country of the roller milling process.

Just as Robert Ransome and his descendants built up their business by producing the implements demanded by innovative farmers, so other companies in the town served the agricultural community either by manufacturing fertilisers for the fields or by processing the products of the farms. The first factory for the manufacture of artificial fertiliser was set up in the late 1840s by Edward Packard, and by 1880 there were five firms in the town and surrounding area engaged in the production of manures. Three of them were in this century to be united under the name of Fison, Packard and Prentice Ltd. and were to become the basis of a world-famous company which in 1973 had a turnover of no less than £150 million.

15.   The first artificial fertiliser factory on the corner of Coprolite Street, a thoroughfare named after the phosphatic nodules that were the original raw material of fertiliser manufacture.

Wheat grown on the fields of rural Suffolk was ground into flour by a score of windmills scattered around the outskirts of the town and by the tidemill which stood on the town side of Stoke Bridge until 1877. The flour produced by these wind and water mills and by the steam mills which replaced them was not only intended for local consumption; large quantities of flour were sent by sea to London, and when a windmill standing beside the Orwell was for sale in the early 19th century it was advertised as having particular advantages for the shipping of its product.

The town's maltings likewise made use of transport by sea both for the reception of barley from the Black Sea and for the outward carriage of malt both to the London breweries and to overseas markets. The growing of fine malting barley on East Anglian farms prompted the very early development of malting in the region, and there is evidence of the industry in Ipswich in medieval times; in the 19th century and the early years of the present century some very large maltings were built by the firm of R. & W. Paul in the dock area.

In this century a sugar factory was constructed between Ipswich and Sproughton for the processing of beet grown on Suffolk farms. And an Ipswich engineering firm, Cocksedge and Co. Ltd., played a significant part in the development of the British sugar industry by making beet-processing equipment for the expanding chain of factories operated by the British Sugar Corporation.

Many of the ships owned by the town's merchants were built in the shipyards which lined the banks of the Orwell, mainly in the parish of St Clement's. At the beginning of the 17th century the town's shipwrights formed themselves into a company which in due course received a charter, and in the 18th century Ipswich shipbuilders were turning out ships for the merchants of London and for the Royal Navy as well as colliers and other vessels for the coastal trade. In the 19th century Jabez Bayley made a name for himself by building the East Indiaman *Orwell* at Halifax Yard, just upstream of Bourne Bridge, and followed that by building two further Indiamen, the *William Fairlie* and *David Scott*, the largest vessels ever built on the Orwell.

Smaller vessels continued to be built until the end of the century, although the construction of the Wet Dock in the 1830s forced those shipbuilders who had yards in that area to move. The last round-bottomed sailing vessel to be built in the town was the brigantine *Clementine*, which came off the ways at the new St Clement's Yard in 1885, but flat-bottomed sailing barges were even then still being built in considerable numbers; the last was the *Ardwina*, built by Orvis and Fuller in 1909. Barges and other vessels are, however, still repaired at Dock End Yard.

The River and Dock

At a time when waterways all over Britain were being improved and canals were being cut to serve the country's growing industries a proposal was made that the Gipping should be made navigable up to Stowmarket, almost seventeen miles inland from Ipswich by river. Faced already with the stagnation of the town's trade because of the deficiencies of the tidal Orwell, the Corporation of Ipswich opposed the proposal to such effect that it was dropped for the time being, to be resurrected in 1789 when William Jessop surveyed the river and reported on how it should be made navigable. The navigation was opened after some initial difficulties in 1793.

Barges carried coal and timber up to Stowmarket, but larger vessels were still unable to reach the quays at Ipswich. The answer to the town's problems would be the damming of the Orwell in Downham Reach and the construction of a lock to admit shipping to the

16.   The Indiaman *Orwell* under construction by Jabez Bayley at Halifax Yard in 1817. Though not the largest vessel built in Ipswich, the *Orwell* attracted great interest; the cost of her building was a factor in Bayley's bankruptcy some years later.

17.   A plan of 1804 showing a proposed new channel to be dredged in the approaches to the town's quays.

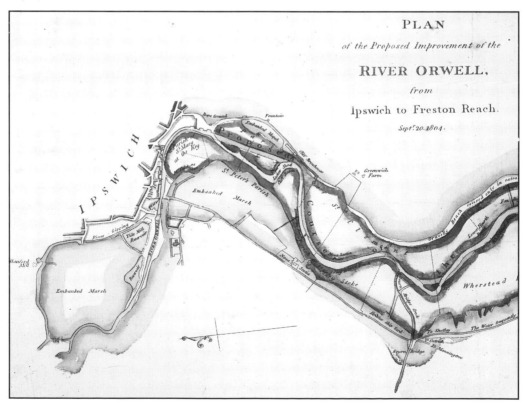

very large non-tidal harbour so formed, reported the engineer William Chapman in 1797. Alas, it was too ambitious a scheme to be taken up, but a later scheme suggested by Chapman met with the approval of River Commissioners appointed under an Act of 1805. Dredging was subsequently carried out by a steam dredger and new channels were cut to improve the approaches to the town.

More drastic measures were needed, however, and in 1837 the Ipswich Dock Commission was set up by the Ipswich Dock Act of that year. The engineer appointed by these commissioners to design the new dock and to oversee its construction was Henry Palmer, who had taken a leading part in the formation of the Institution of Civil Engineers.

The dock scheme was an enterprising one that was to play a vital part in promoting the town's 19th-century prosperity. Palmer's idea was to close off the river just below Stoke Bridge and at another point further downstream, thus isolating an elbow of river which was to form an enclosed Wet Dock; a new channel taking a more direct course than the old river was to be dug to carry the waters of the Gipping towards the sea. Entry to the dock was by way of a lock linking the New Cut, as the bypass channel was named, and the dock; lock gates retained the water in the dock whatever the state of the tide in the river outside. The first stone of this lock was laid with considerable ceremony in 1839 and the Wet Dock, then the largest area of enclosed water of its kind in Britain, was formally opened in 1842.

When Ransomes were expanding in the 1830s it was a site beside the river that was chosen for them by William Worby, their far-sighted works manager. The gasworks set up in 1821 was already on a riverside site, and so were other commercial and industrial concerns. All were to benefit greatly from the opening of the dock, which was soon thronged with sailing ships of all kinds bringing coal from the Tyne and Wear, timber from the Baltic, pig iron from South Wales and grain from the Black Sea, and loading the products of the town's mills and maltings for carriage to London and elsewhere.

A favourite stroll for the townspeople of Victorian Ipswich was along the Promenade, a pleasant right-of-way alongside the New Cut with a fine view of the ships lying in the new dock. They took a great interest in the shipping, whose masts and yards seemed to tower above them as they wandered through the avenue of limes on a sunny Sunday morning or stood to chat to their friends and acquaintances under the shelter of the 'Umbrella', an open building at the east end of the Promenade.

With the increasing size of ships using the port it became necessary to replace the original entrance by a new and much larger lock in a more suitable position; the lower dam forming the Wet Dock was cut through to accommodate the 300-ft. lock, and a new channel was dredged to give access to it. The new lock was opened on 27 July 1881, when the paddle steamer *Glen Rosa*, carrying a large number of local and national dignitaries, was the first vessel to pass through. On the same day the new post office on Cornhill and the new museum in High Street were opened.

By the turn of the century even the 1881 lock was proving inadequate and in 1912 plans were made for its replacement by an even larger lock capable of handling large steamers as well as the sailing vessels which made up the great majority of ships trading through the port in the 1870s and 1880s. The outbreak of war in 1914 overtook this scheme, and since the 1920s the port has expanded outside the Wet Dock, which is now used less by commercial shipping than by yachts. The busy quays of the Port of Ipswich now extend along both sides of the Orwell where once were extensive mudflats and a beach popular with the town's youngsters.

18. A small vessel waiting to enter the Wet Dock from the New Cut; a photograph taken by Richard Dykes Alexander in the 1850s. In the foreground are the gates of the entrance lock.

19. The paddle steamer *Glen Rosa* passing through the new lock on the opening day, 27 July 1881.

Social History

'The big village era has passed away; that of the large town commenced', commented the *East Anglian Daily Times*, which had commenced publication in the town in 1874, when in 1881 the new lock, the new post office and the new museum were all opened on the same day. Indeed, Ipswich was changing, though it can hardly be true to say that it had ever been merely a large village.

At the time of the first Census in 1801 there were 11,277 living in the town, most of them within the medieval ramparts and within the ancient parishes immediately outside, but by 1851 the population had risen to almost 33,000. The majority of the newcomers were country people attracted by the prospect of employment in the town's thriving industries. Some of them could find accommodation only in what William Hunt in 1864 called 'wretched plaster huts, such as only the descendants of the inhabitants of the squalid part of old towns would consent to live in' or in insanitary courts where the air was 'poisoned by foul emanations from drains and sewers' and the drinking water was drawn from wells polluted by leakage from the adjacent cesspools.

Those more fortunate lived in new houses which were erected in new streets beyond the limits of the old town. Between 1831 and 1841 the number of houses rose from 4,116 to 5,240, and in the next decade it rose by another 1,739. Further expansion of the town later in the century was promoted by organisations such as the Ipswich and Suffolk Freehold Land Society, formed in 1849 'to improve the social position and promote the moral elevation of the unenfranchised population of this country'. The first purchase made by the Freehold Land Society (now the Ipswich Building Society) was the Cauldwell Hall estate, which was divided into 282 allotments selling at £21 10s. 0d. each. William Hunt wrote of 'that California of heterogeneous small freeholds', and California was indeed the name by which the area became known, though today it is more often referred to as St John's from the dedication of the parish church, established in 1857.

The first president of the Freehold Land Society was Richard Dykes Alexander, a Quaker banker who was foremost among those who pressed in the 1830s for the improvement of facilities for trade and became chairman of the Ipswich Dock Commission. Alexander was one of the first people in the district to espouse photography as a hobby, and some of the photographs that reflect his practical philanthropy appear in this book. He was much concerned with the Ragged School movement and with similar institutions, and is said to have built the Temperance Hall at the corner of High Street and Crown Street at his own expense.

Ipswich was singularly blessed with men whose philanthropy took a practical turn. Ransomes established a relief society for their workers which became known as the 'Old Sick Fund' as early as 1817 and provided a workmen's hall in the late 1840s, besides supporting the town's Mechanics' Institute, founded in 1824 and still in existence as the Ipswich Institute in Tavern Street. And Daniel Ford Goddard, later to be knighted, established the Social Settlement in 1896 as an undenominational and non-political community centre providing some essential social services at a time when the Welfare State was hardly even a dream in the minds of radical reformers.

Richard Dykes Alexander lived in a large house on the corner of St Matthew's Street and Mill Street (now Portman Road) which is still standing as part of the telephone exchange. Others who made their fortunes in industry or commerce in the town built themselves 'residences which, if they do not rival in quaint oak carving, the dwellings which the merchant princes of Ipswich built for themselves in the lower part of the town in Elizabethan days, more than equal them in dignity, in boldness of architecture, in

20. Richard Dykes Alexander: banker, philanthropist and pioneer photographer.

21. Richard Dykes Alexander and two of his family in the garden of his house, St Matthew's.

22. Old houses on the Carnser in Stoke Street, 1896. At the door on the left are shoemaker Mr. Garner and his wife. These houses all came down to make way for the People's Hall, begun in 1898.

spaciousness, and in their adaptation to the comfort and enjoyment of the residents'. Hunt refers to Fonnereau Road, formed in 1847 on the western boundary of Christchurch Park (rather reluctantly bought by the town's Corporation in 1894), as 'part of a handsome modern suburb' with 'many suburban houses and gardens ... occupied by manufacturers, merchants, and other leading inhabitants of the town'.

Life was pleasant in these suburban houses, but it was far less pleasant for those who were euphemistically termed 'the poorer classes', for whom all kinds of charities were set up, including the Society for Encouragement of Industry whose object was 'to provide needlework during the winter months for poor women at their own homes, paying them for their labour'.

For those who lived in the dilapidated cottages that made up so much of the town's housing life could be hard – and short. When Dr. G. S. Elliston, the town's first Medical Officer of Health, made his first report in 1874 he revealed that out of every hundred children born in the town no fewer than 26 died before reaching the age of five.

Twentieth-century Changes
With the turn of the century the pace of change in Ipswich accelerated. More and more old buildings came down in the interests of road widening or to make way for new shops such as the Ipswich Industrial Co-operative Society's central premises in Carr Street which were expanded in 1908, 1915 and 1928.

23. Flint and brick cottages built in the mid-19th century in California. Some were built at the rear of the plot with long front gardens which were virtually smallholdings.

In 1903 the old horse trams gave way to electric trams, and these were replaced between 1923 and 1926 by electric trolleybuses, some of them made in Ipswich by Ransomes, Sims & Jefferies. Motor buses were not seen on town services until 1950, though they took over entirely from the trolleybuses in 1963.

In the 1930s a great many of the older houses which had become run down and insanitary were cleared away, their residents being rehoused in neat homes newly erected on estates ringing the periphery of the town. In 1934 an official publication claimed that one house in every five had been built in the past 10 years and that almost five thousand new houses had been built in the twenties; almost a third of them had been provided by the local authority.

After the Second World War reconstruction proceeded apace, and in the sixties there came a scheme for the forced expansion of the town to a population of 200,000, representing an approximate doubling in size. That scheme was eventually dropped by the government of the day, which decreed that instead Ipswich should be allowed to grow more naturally, but nevertheless the radical plans drawn up by Shankland Cox had had their effect on thinking in the town for some years. The Greyfriars development was one unhappy result.

THE MEDIEVAL TOWN

24. The West Gate formed part of the 13th-century defences of the town, though it was not built until much later than the bank and ditch, authorised in 1203. The lower part of the gate dated from the latter part of the 14th century, the upper part from a 15th-century rebuilding. The gate was demolished in 1781.

25.   The remains of the Blackfriars monastery between Foundation Street and Fore Street as they appeared in the mid-18th century. The Dominican friars arrived in Ipswich in 1263 and in the course of the following hundred years acquired extensive property in the town on which a large church and other buildings were erected.

26.   William Vick's photograph of the ruins of the Priory of St Peter and St Paul in Foundation Street, taken about 1880.

27. Houses built on the town bank in Old Foundry Road. The medieval defences seem never to have consisted of more than a bank and ditch with a palisade along the top of the ramparts. Old Foundry Road was in the 18th century known as St Margaret's Ditches, as the road ran along the town ditch.

28. Nineteenth-century houses on the earthen bank in Tower Ramparts, a name which survives even though all trace of the bank has gone.

29. The bounds of the parishes were all-important in days when much of the administration was parochial. This boundary stone marked the limits of St Clement's parish which formerly extended over a considerable extra-mural area east of the town.

30. Tower Street took its name from the church of St Mary-le-Tower, for many years the principal parish church of Ipswich. The original church, seen here in one of William Vick's pictures, was a medieval building with a spire. This spire fell during a hurricane in 1661, doing a great deal of damage to the church.

31. The Old Coffee House at the corner of Tower Street and Tavern Street was a fine 16th-century town house well known for its decorative cornerpost and other carved adornments. The front of the house was sacrificed in 1817 in the interests of road widening, and the building has since been entirely demolished; the British Home Stores now occupies the site.

NINETEENTH-CENTURY EXPANSION

32. The parish church of one of the medieval extra-mural suburbs. St Helen's was largely rebuilt in the 19th century to accommodate the 'large, poor and fast-increasing population', to quote an appeal for funds issued by the rector and churchwardens.

33. Old Waterloo House was the original home of the Footman enterprise, now Debenhams, established in 1815. The prefix 'old' was added when Footman's moved into a new Waterloo House in Westgate Street. By the lamp-post is the entrance to Mumford's Passage, leading to Tower Ramparts.

34. With the population increasing fast and prosperity returning, the 19th century saw new streets being built through what had been gardens. Museum Street was laid out in 1847-48 and the Methodist Church seen here was built in 1861. On the right can be seen the Tuscan columns of the museum designed by Christopher Fleury in 1847.

35. The Eastern Union Railway reached Ipswich in 1846, the first station being built on the site later occupied by the locomotive depot. To carry the line on to Bury St Edmunds and Norwich, the engineer Peter Bruff drove a tunnel through Stoke Hill, and in 1860 a new station was opened at the north end of the tunnel.

36. The view northwards from Stoke Hill showing the railway goods yard laid out on reclaimed land where the tidal pond for Stoke Mill had once been. In the middle of the picture, taken in 1887, can be seen E. R. & F. Turner's Greyfriars Works.

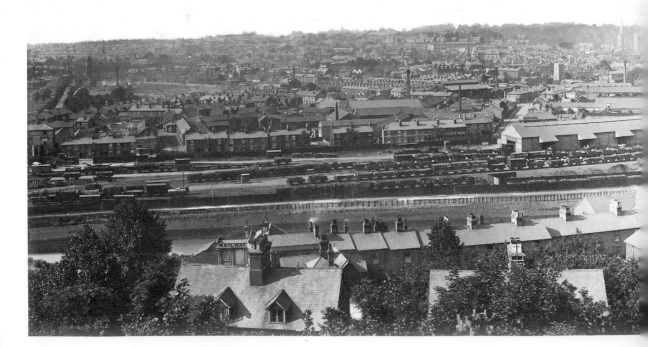

37. A photograph of the new station, looking towards the tunnel, taken by William Vick some time before 1883 when the island platform was added.

38. Looking from Stoke Hill towards the dock, 1887. The prominent Salvation Army barracks in Burrell Road were opened in 1884; they were the subject of violent attacks in their early years.

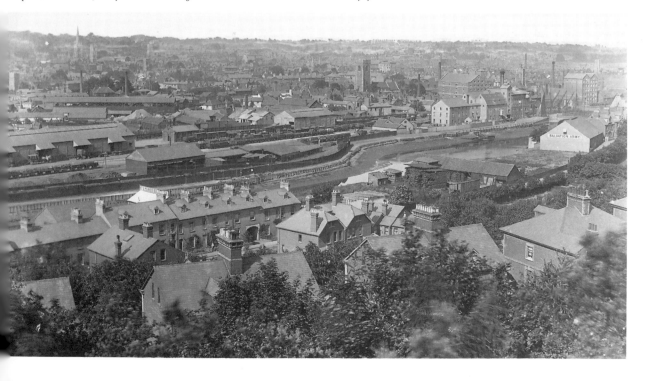

J. HEPWORTH & SON, OF LEEDS.
WATERLOO HOUSE
WHOLESALE CLOTHING AND HAT MANUFACTURERS.

39. Cornhill in Victorian times. William Vick took this photograph of the crowds watching the procession which celebrated Queen Victoria's golden jubilee on 21 June 1887. Within a few years, many of the buildings on the north side of Cornhill had been replaced by a much more imposing block in red brick.

40.   The first Ipswich postmaster, Jason Grover, organised a regular postal service in the 1620s, some years before the General Post Office was established. The new post office on Cornhill, built by the Corporation in 1881, still serves as the town's head post office.

41.   Cornhill about 1898, showing the ornate block of buildings which replaced Old Waterloo House and other shops seen in plate 39. The horse trams had arrived in 1880.

42. The horse tram depot in Quadling Street survived long after the closure of the system in 1903. The tram shed has now been demolished, but there are hopes that it might be re-erected in a proposed Ipswich Transport Museum.

43. Tramcar No. 9 at Derby Road. The line from Major's Corner to Derby Road station opened in 1883, but it was only linked to the rest of the system at the Cornhill the following year. Opposition to the tramway was not beaten by this extension, and a tradesman managed to hold up a tram in Carr Street with his horse and trap for no less than 28 minutes.

44. In the 19th century and right up to the 1920 the economy of a town like Ipswich depended greatly on the horse for transport. Around the turn of the century Joseph Bird & Son were coal merchants at Stoke Bridge and brickmakers at the Trinity Brick Works in Cavendish Street.

45. The Central Livery and Bait Stables erected by Fred Smith & Company early this century still stand in Princes Street, though they have not catered for horses for very many years. Other livery stables included the Old West End Posting Establishment, where jobmaster George Fenn advertised well-appointed horses and traps at moderate charges: 'Commercial Gentlemen contracted for'.

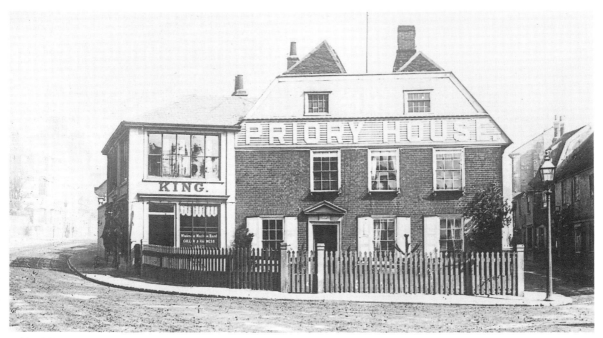

46. Many ancillary trades served the horse economy. George King at Priory House on the corner of Princes Street and Friars Street was a saddler and harnessmaker.

47. King's premises made way for the warehouse of Grimwade, Ridley & Company, wholesale druggists and colour merchants, but the horse in the shafts remained a familiar sight.

48. The kilns of one of R. & W. Paul's dockside maltings are prominent in this bird's-eye view of the dock area at the beginning of the century. The Customs House and St Clement's Church also feature in the view.

49. The rooftops of Ipswich seen from the Town Hall in 1868. R. M. Phipson's rebuilding of St Mary-le-Tower is well under way and the new spire is prominent in the middle of the picture, but St Lawrence's 15th-century tower on the right has not yet been rebuilt; it was heightened in 1882 by Frederick Barnes and H. Gaye.

50. The English Presbyterian Church, now Barrack Corner United Reformed Church, was built in 1870 by Frederick Barnes, who contributed so much to the Ipswich scene. Like other churches of the period it has walls of Kentish ragstone, brought to Ipswich by barge.

51. The earliest of the Ipswich free churches, the Unitarian Meeting House in Friars Street, was erected in 1699-1700 by a carpenter, Joseph Clarke. A timber-framed and plastered building, it has much in common with the churches of New England, set up by East Anglians who dared to hold the view that a church was no more sacred than any other building.

52. The interior of Museum Street Methodist Church, a photograph taken in the early years of this century. The layout is typical of 19th-century Wesleyan chapels.

53. William Vick's photograph of the interior of the English Presbyterian Church, taken soon after its opening.

54.   Sunday School teachers of St Nicholas Street Independent Chapel, later known as St Nicholas Baptist Church. The photograph was taken *c*.1890.

55. The choir of St Mary-le-Tower Church in 1880: yet another example of William Vick's work.

56. St Mary-le-Tower was totally rebuilt by R. M. Phipson between 1860 and 1870. Writing in 1864, William Hunt said that 'the work that has already been done to the structure, and to its adornment outside and in, is of an elaborate description, and was executed at enormous expense'.

57. The corner of Carr Street and Upper Brook Street taken by William Vick early one morning in 1888.

58. The same corner two years later, with the new Victoria House premises of George Thomas Pick, linen draper and hosier. Similar transformations were taking place elsewhere in the town.

TRADE AND COMMERCE

59. Window shopping was a Victorian pastime, but the stance of the top-hatted gentleman suggests that he has braced himself against the window frame so as not to move while the lengthy exposure is made. The shop is probably that of Schulen and Boby, watch and clock makers, jewellers and opticians, on Cornhill.

60. Carboys filled with coloured liquids in the window of J. A. Symonds' shop. In the 1860s tradesmen with premises in the Buttermarket decided to widen the east end of the street. After they 'had succeeded in inducing the Local Board of Health to vote £2,000 for the piece of land to be thrown into the street, [they] purchased the whole line of property and replaced the low and antiquated premises with the row of lofty and good-looking white and red brick houses' of which this is one.

61. Upper Brook Street at the turn of the century with William Henry Marsh, chemist and druggist, at the door of No. 37. Symonds' shop projects at the corner of the Buttermarket.

62. Looking down on the Buttermarket corner, with Joseph Squirrell's 'Very Centre Stores' next door to the *Cock and Pye* on the other side of Upper Brook Street.

63. One of the town's windmills in Tower Mill Road, off Bramford Road, gave its name to the Tower Mill Steam Laundry. Collection and delivery was, of course, by horse-drawn van.

64.   Fruit and potato merchant Thomas Henry Smith, on the left, helping to unload a consignment of oranges at his shop in Upper Orwell Street. The barrels behind Mr. Smith contain Jersey potatoes.

65. Bridge Street, Stoke, with Dunnett's fruit shop and the kilns of the malting then belonging to Joseph Fison & Co Ltd. The malting has now been converted into flats.

66. A close-up of William Thomas Dunnett's shop at 3 Bridge Street, Stoke.

7. In the days before milk bottles the milk was delivered by handcart and ladled into the customer's jug. William Wright Hunt was both a dairyman and fruiterer in 1912, but after the 1914-18 war the firm was trading as Alnesbourne Dairies and Bakeries.

68. E. R. George's shop and bake office on the corner of Crown Street and Fonnereau Road seem to have disappeared soon after this photograph, which bears the date 1911, was taken. One of the advertisements is for Poole's Picture Palace in Tower Street, the town's first cinema, which opened in 1909.

69. 'This view presents a commingling of the present and the past', commented William Vick on this view of Tavern Street about 1890. Tavern Street took its name from the many taverns, including the *Mitre*, which occupied premises in the street.

70. (*Left*) George Barnard's coffee house at 42 St Margaret's Street, an alternative to the taverns selling intoxicating liquor. Next door at No. 44 lived John Spencer, 'chimney cleaner'.

71. (*Below*) After earlier unsuccessful efforts to found a co-operative society in the town, the Ipswich Industrial Co-operative Society began trading in 1869 in premises in Carr Street. The Foxhall Road branch shown here was opened in 1906.

72. The Ipswich Gas Light Company was formed in 1821, four years after the first gas-producing plant had been brought into use in a corner of Robert Ransome's foundry. The company was approaching its 90th anniversary when the employees gathered in the works to have their photograph taken.

73. Gas company employees wore a workmanlike uniform which included stiff collar and tie as well as overalls.

74. The company built a gasworks on land that it bought beside the Orwell, handy for the supply of coal by sea. The sailing barges seen alongside the gasworks quay in this picture of about 1920 are unloading coal for the works.

75.   The cattle market, held on a site in Princes Street from 1856 until the 1980s, brought many country people into Ipswich. Often families did their shopping in the town while the menfolk were at the market or in the Corn Exchange.

76.   Farmers and corn merchants doing business in the Corn Exchange. The advertisement on the wall is for Meux's beers, brewed in London 'from Suffolk and Essex barleys malted in Ipswich'. The firm had a large maltings between Fore Street and the dock.

77. Carriers' carts like this one operated by Charles Mayhew were the country people's link with the town. Mayhew came into Ipswich from Manningtree on Tuesdays (market day) and Fridays, making his base at the *Coach and Horses* in Upper Brook Street.

78. The first bus services in the Ipswich area were operated by the Great Eastern Railway, which in 1905 began running buses between Ipswich station and Shotley Pier. One of the railway buses is seen here at Ipswich station about 1912. The railway interest in the Shotley route was bought out by the Eastern Counties Road Car Company in 1922.

79.   More like the carrier's cart that preceded it than the country bus of later years, Harry Watkins' lorry waits on St Margaret's Green for the time of its return to Framsden. It ran every day in the 1920s except Wednesdays and Sundays.

80.   Major's Corner about 1920 showing the garage of Botwoods Ltd. In the last century Botwoods had been coachmakers, producing all kinds of vehicles, including rickshaws, for export to the colonies.

81. A Tilling-Stevens bus supplied to the Eastern Counties Road Car Company in 1926, seen operating the Ipswich-Shotley service.

82. Country buses operated by the Eastern Counties Omnibus Co. Ltd., successors to the Road Car Company, seen at the Old Cattle Market in the early 1930s.

INDUSTRY

33.   The only known illustration of Robert
Ransome's foundry in St Margaret's Ditches is
this painting of the skittle alley that lay behind
the foundry. On the roof is a wooden sign in the
shape of a ploughshare.

34.   The Ransomes, Sims & Jefferies stand at
the British Empire Exhibition in Buenos Aires
in 1930. Ransomes' export trade had peaked just
before the 1914-18 war, but the export of
agricultural implements remained important
and exhibiting at such shows proved a valuable
means of obtaining orders.

85. An invoice of 1842 for a patent 'Albert' plough supplied to the Prince Consort on behalf of Queen Victoria following the visit to Windsor Castle by Theophilus Smith of Attleborough, who discussed the Ransomes plough with Prince Albert.

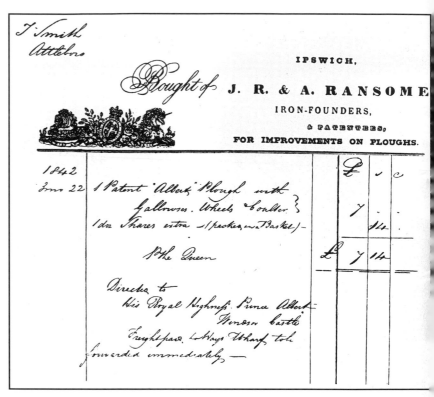

86. A page from an 1859 catalogue issued by Ransomes & Sims, as the Ransomes business was then titled. Early ploughing engines designed by John Fowler, who later established his own works in Leeds, were built by Ransomes & Sims in Ipswich.

87.   Ransomes' workers with one of the FE2b fighter aircraft produced at the 'White City' in Fore Hamlet for the Royal Flying Corps in 1917-18. The hangars in which they were built had been hastily erected to enable the company to undertake aircraft construction. They later became the company's lawnmower works.

88.   The Prince of Wales (later Duke of Windsor) is presented with a Motrac tractor plough for use on his Canadian ranch during a visit to Ransomes' Orwell Works on 26 June 1930.

89.   A metal advertising sign for Ransomes' ploughs, illustrating four of the many different types made at the Orwell Works.

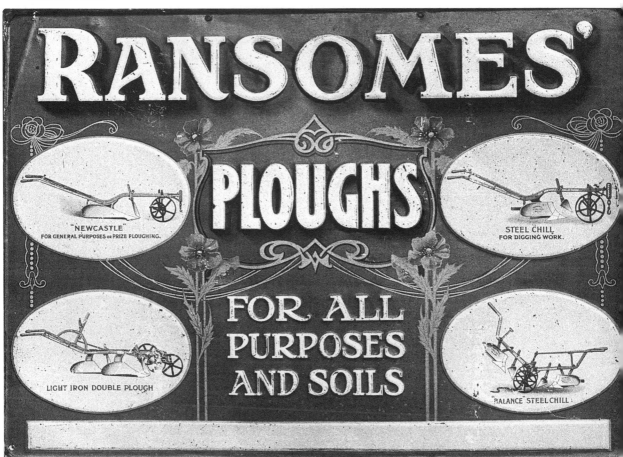

90. Ransomes' plough works at a time when the production of tractor-mounted ploughs was in full swing.

91. Made by Ransomes & Rapier, this steam-powered concrete mixer had an engine and boiler made by Ransomes, Sims & Jefferies.

92. (*Above*) When Richard Rapier constructed the first railway in China, the Shanghai and Woosung Tramway, two engines were built at Waterside Works for the line. One of them, the *Flowery Land*, is seen at the works before being shipped overseas.

93. (*Facing page*) A steam carriage made by Ransomes & Rapier in the 1870s for use on a colonial railway, illustrated on a page from *Little Railways*, a promotional book published by the company in 1880.

94. (*Below*) A 45-ton steam breakdown crane built by Ransomes & Rapier about 1940 for the Southern Railway seen outside Waterside Works awaiting delivery.

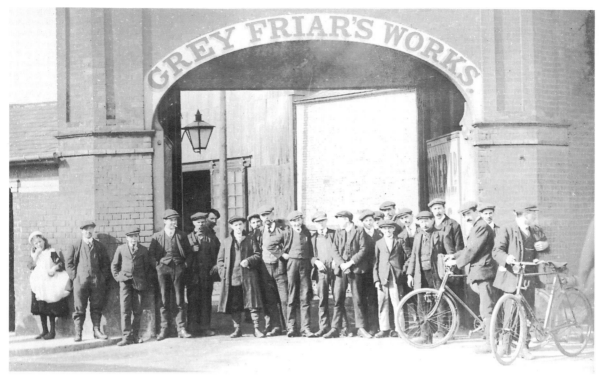

95. E. R. & F. Turner had two works in Ipswich in the early part of the century: Greyfriars Works, shown here, and St Peter's Ironworks near Stoke Bridge. Turner's were pioneers of the roller milling process and fitted up many mills in East Anglia and further afield, building the steam engine to power the milling plant as well as the plant itself.

96. Employees leaving Ransomes' Orwell Works at dinner time on 18 November 1904. The company employed some 2,500 men and boys at this period, a particularly prosperous one for the works.

'VICTORIA' COOKING RANGE.

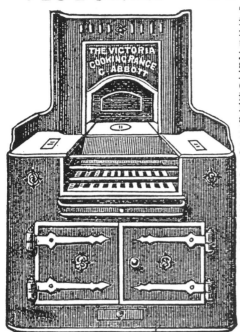

OPEN

THIS Range has, since its introduction, come very rapidly into favour with those requiring a Cheap, yet thoroughly strong, serviceable and durable Range. It has Open and Close Fire as shown by illustrations, with excellent Draught, exceptionally large oven; will Cook Large or Small Joints, Bread, Pastry, &c., requiring very little attention. The improved construction of the Oven insures perfect cleanliness, it being impossible for any dirt or soot to find its way through. It is very easily fixed, and is generally admitted by practical men to be the Best and Cheapest of its class yet offered.

REGD TRADE MARK.

THE "ABBOTT"

PRICES
FROM 30/- EACH,
ACCORDING TO SIZE.

Awarded GOLD MEDAL & DIPLOMA,

Ipswich Trades' Exhibition, 1895,

For Excellence of Victoria and other Ranges.

RANGES, BOILERS, AND STOVES
Of all Descriptions Repaired on the Shortest Notice.

LAWN MOWERS of all Makers, and every description of Agricultural Implements Repaired and made Equal to New at very Reasonable Cost.

PALISADING, GATES, TOMBS, RAILINGS, &c., Cast and Fixed to Order.
SMITHS' and BUILDERS' WORK in all its Branches at Low Prices.
LOCKS Repaired, and KEYS fitted to same on the Shortest Notice.

GEORGE ABBOTT,
NEW CROWN STREET WORKS,
CORNER OF HIGH STREET AND CROWN STREET,
IPSWICH.

---

97. Ransomes was by no means the only foundry in Ipswich. This advertisement from the *Suffolk County Handbook* for 1896 shows some of the products of a firm based at the Crown Street Ironworks, which had begun life in 1840 as the Temperance Hall.

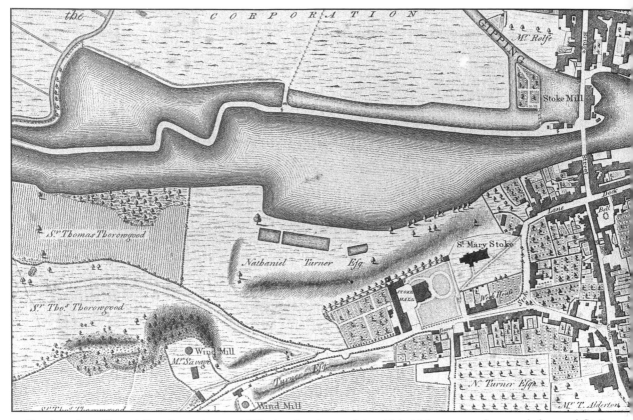

98. A section of Joseph Pennington's map, 1778, showing the ponds in which tidal water was impounded to work Stoke Mill. The two windmills on Stoke Hill can also be seen.

99. Stoke Bridge and the tidemill in 1790, with a single windmill visible on Stoke Hill. The tidemill was moved from this position by hydraulic power on 1 September 1877; in spite of its appearance in this print it was a timber-framed and weatherboarded building.

100. The building with the mansard roof on the left of this 19th-century photograph of Stoke Bridge is the former tidemill in its new position, now forming part of the Eastern Union Mills complex. The cast-iron Stoke Bridge had been built by Ransomes in 1818 to a design by William Cubitt (later Sir William), who became engineer to Ransomes in 1812.

101. Stoke windmill was almost the last survivor of the score or more windmills in and around Ipswich which had ground grain for local consumption and for shipping to London.

102. The foreman maltster in Paul's Stoke maltings tests the green malt on the floor.

103. Steam rises from the kilns of the Stoke maltings on a we morning. These were built in the first decade of this century and closed down about 1980, having been superseded by more modern types of malting.

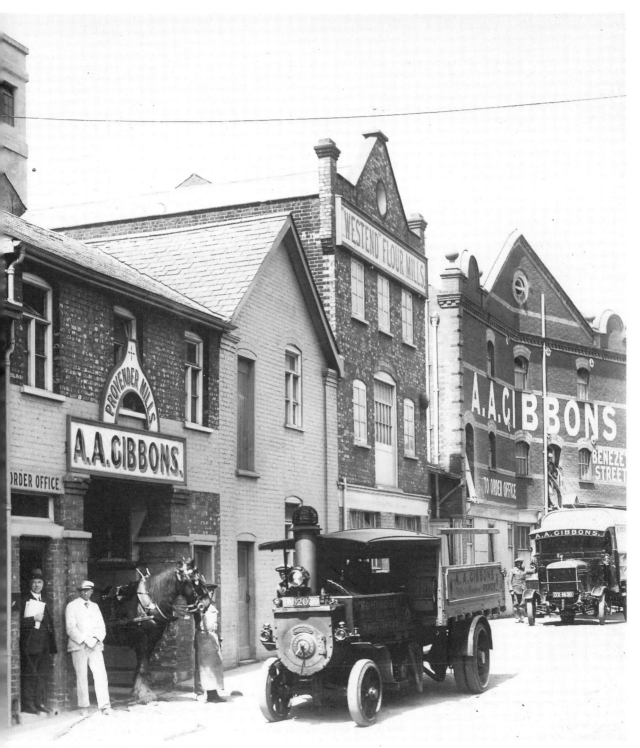

104.   The Westend Flour Mills of A. A. Gibbons in Benezet Street in the 1920s, when the company used both steam waggons and motor lorries for their deliveries. Alfred Alexander Gibbons had begun business in Benezet Street as a corn merchant in the 1880s.

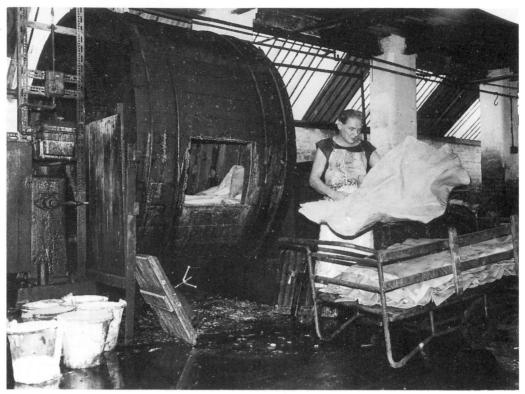

105. Skins being removed from one of the tanning drums at the Bramford Road tannery of
W. & A. J. Turner, now closed down. Tanning had been carried on in Ipswich for centuries;
archaeologists have found evidence of leather working even in the Saxon town.

106. There is no record of what kind of machinery was used to harness the water of the Gipping to
power Henry Knights' printing machines at his works in Princes Street, where he produced the
weekly *Ipswich Journal*. When the newspaper office moved to Museum Street in 1890 Knights seems
to have moved his printing works to Falcon Street.

PRINTING BY STEAM AND WATER POWER.

Bible and Crown Printing Works,
PRINCES STREET, IPSWICH.

HENRY KNIGHTS,

(Publisher of the Ipswich Journal and Knights's County Handbook)

EXECUTES EVERY DESCRIPTION OF

LETTER-PRESS PRINTING

NEATLY AND EXPEDITIOUSLY, AND ON THE MOST REASONABLE TERMS.

Orders received as above, or (by permission of the Proprietor) at the "Ipswich Journal" Office, Ipswich.

107. There is a long history of printing in Ipswich. This is the composing room of W. E. Harrison & Sons' Ancient House Press, situated behind the Ancient House in the Buttermarket, in the early years of this century.

108. The press room at the Ancient House Press, with its three flat-bed printing machines. The Ancient House became a bookshop in the mid-19th century, and the printing business developed as an adjunct of the bookselling and stationery business.

109. Mr. S. H. Cowell established a printing works in 1818 which grew until it occupied a large area between the Buttermarket and Falcon Street, with Old Market Lane running alongside. In 1900 the company became W. S. Cowell Ltd. Today the printing works has moved outside the town centre and the site is being redeveloped as a shopping precinct.

110. The corset manufacturing business of Footman, Pretty & Nicholson was founded in 1820 and in the third quarter of the 19th century began to expand rapidly. A new factory was built in Tower Ramparts in 1882, and from 1889 the business was carried on as William Pretty & Sons. The factory was demolished in the 1980s.

THE RIVER AND DOCK

111. Loading a sailing barge on the foreshore of the Orwell from a waggon. This picture was taken in the late 1850s by Robert Burrows (1810-83), an Ipswich artist who developed an interest in photography around the mid-1850s.

112. A brig, a schooner, a billyboy and other shipping in the dock: another photograph by Robert Burrows. The warehouse in the left background is one of those designed by Henry Palmer, who reported to the Dock Commissioners in 1838 that 'it is proposed to support the front walls of the warehouses upon a Colonade, the Columns being composed of Cast Iron'.

113. Shipping in Ipswich Dock in the 1860s, photographed by Richard Dykes Alexander. In the background is the fertiliser factory on the corner of Coprolite Street.

114. Sailing barges anchored in the Orwell about the turn of the century. On the left is a schooner on the slip at the Cliff Shipyard, which disappeared when Cliff Quay was built in 1923.

115. Griffin Wharf seen across the New Cut in a photograph taken by Richard Dykes Alexander about 1859, showing the 'drop' from which coke from the adjoining coke ovens was loaded into barges.

116. The Customs House and shipping in the dock about 1880. The tower of St Clement's Church can be seen just to the right of the Customs House, which was designed by J. M. Clark and opened in 1844.

117. Unloading barges in the dock about 1890. Above the rooftops can be seen the kilns of R. & W. Paul's dockside maltings.

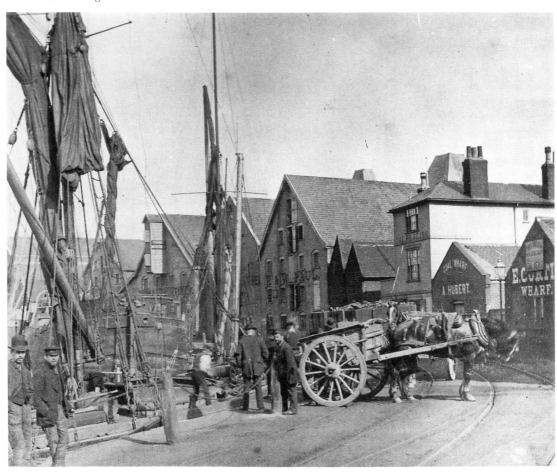

118. The 'Umbrella' at the eastern end of the Promenade, seen in a photograph taken by William Vick about 1880. A favourite resort of the townspeople, the Promenade disappeared when the Dock Commissioners extended their facilities in this century.

119. Excavation of the new lock under way in 1880. Considerable difficulties were experienced by the contractors, Henry Lee & Son, because of the unstable nature of the chalk just above foundation level and the constant flooding by springs in the overlying gravel. A barrow run by which excavated material was removed can be seen rising to the right-hand side.

120.   The paddle steamer *Orwell*, a successor to vessels of the same name built in 1815 and 1839, sails down the New Cut on her way to Harwich in a well-known photograph by Harry Walters.

121.   The boomie barge *Ethel Edith*, owned at the time by Robert Peck of Great Whip Street, Ipswich, and several spritsail barges passing through the 1881 lock into the dock about the turn of the century. The *Ethel Edith* was built at Ipswich in 1892.

122. The little spritsail barge *Fairy* unloading in Ipswich dock. Built on the Thames in 1861, she was owned by William Groom of Harwich.

123. Unloading Australian wheat from the barque *Penang* in 1933. It will be lightered up to the mills at the head of the dock by the sailing barge into which the sacks are being emptied.

124. Ipswich Dock in 1936, seen under the bows of the barque *Killoran*, which had brought 2,991 tons of Australian wheat. One of F. T. Everard & Sons' steam coasters is unloading coal at Mellonie & Goulder's wharf, while R. & W. Paul's big coasting barge *Barbara Jean*, lost at Dunkirk four years later, sails up the dock.

125.   The dock in the 1970s, with a coaster discharging fertiliser at Eastern Counties Farmers' silo in the foreground. The pontoon crane and the gantry just beyond were used for handling aggregate dredged from the River Stour.

126.   Pitchpine logs being unloaded from the S.S. *Regina* in Ipswich Dock in 1910. The logs are being dropped into the water and taken to one of the timber ponds which used to occupy the area between the dock and the New Cut.

SOCIAL HISTORY

127. The Ipswich Ragged School began operations in 1849 in an attempt to provide a modicum of education for the child 'too poor, too ragged, too filthy, too ignorant, for ordinary instruction'. Richard Dykes Alexander provided the money to set up the school, and it was he who in 1859 took these pictures of the master, Joshua Newman, instructing some of his pupils in carpentry.

128. Joshua Newman and some of the pupils standing outside the 'purpose-built' schoolroom opened in 1858 to house the Ipswich Ragged School.

129. (*Above*) Those more fortunate could go to the Grammar School, which can trace its history back to the early years of the 15th century. In 1853 the school moved to new premises designed by Christopher Fleury on what were then the outskirts of the town.

130. (*Left*) Christ's Hospital at one time shared with the Grammar School a home in the old Blackfriars, and in 1883 its endowments were merged with those of what has now become known as Ipswich School. This photograph by Vick shows the Christ's Hospital Boarding School in Wherstead Road just a few years before the merger.

131. (*Right*) The Ipswich School Board, set up under the Education Act of 1870, provided a number of new schools including one in Bramford Road, now the home of the Suffolk Record Office. Opened in 1882, the school was quite new when photographed by William Vick.

132. One of the first schools provided by the school board was that in Wherstead Road, built in 1872 'for 702 boys, girls and infants'. With the takeover in 1903 by the Ipswich Local Education Authority, the school was enlarged to accommodate more than a thousand pupils.

133. In 1898 Mr. H. W. Packard presented a challenge shield to be competed for by 'The Public Elementary Boys' Schools of Ipswich for Highest Per Centage of School Attendance'. The winners here are a class from Clifford Road school.

134.   A class at the Ipswich High School for Girls in the former Assembly Rooms in Northgate Street in the 1880s. The school, established by the Girls' Public Day School Trust, moved from Northgate Street to Westerfield Road in 1907.

135. Lord Kitchener, who had been appointed High Steward of Ipswich in 1909, attended a Boy Scouts' rally at Portman Road on 31 May 1911. His visit was considered of sufficient interest for it to be filmed for showing at one of the local cinemas.

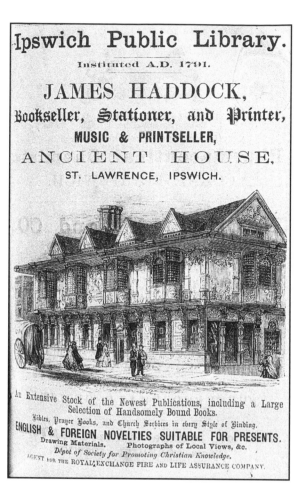

136. James Haddock at the Ancient House in the Buttermarket n only sold books but operated the Ipswich public library, which i 1892 was said to contain about 16,000 volumes.

137. The upstairs room in which the library was housed is seen i this photograph by William Vick. Besides the public library, th Ancient House also maintained a medical library established i 1824.

138. The Ipswich Museum was established in 1847 in the street to which it gave its name, and from the outset it was intended that it should be 'more particularly for the benefit of the working classes'. Unfortunately the lectures given regularly at the museum, 'to which tickets for free admission are distributed among the working classes', failed to attract the attention of more than a minority of such people.

139. In 1881 an imposing new museum in High Street, designed by Horace Cheston, was opened. To one side was a school of art which, like the museum, continues in operation today.

140. The Ipswich Institute, which since 1834 has occupied premises in Tavern Street, began life in 1824 as the Mechanics' Institution, with the object of instructing 'the members in the principles of the arts they practise ... and in the various branches of science and useful knowledge'. This subscriber's receipt is dated 1898.

IPSWICH INSTITUTE.

SUBSCRIBER'S RECEIPT. *Aug 2* 1898.

Received of Mr. *J. J. King*

THREE SHILLINGS, *his Quarterly Subscription due the 1st Wednesday in July, 1898.*

—3s.— A. C. CALVER, Collector.

CLEAR TO THE FIRST WEDNESDAY IN OCTOBER, 1898.

☞ *Any Member desirous of leaving the Institute, must give notice to the SECRETARY (in writing) of his intention TWO WEEKS before the Quarter day at which he proposes to leave, or he will still be considered a Member, and liable to the usual Subscriptions.*

141. Those who refused to avail themselves of the opportunity presented by the museum and the Ipswich Institute might well land up in the prison behind the County Hall in St Helen's Street, which had its beginnings in 1786, was extensively altered in 1883 and later considerably enlarged. Here the prison staff pc for their photograph in December 1909.

142. Founded in 1896 by Daniel Ford Goddard, the Social Settlement at first occupied these rather ancient premises in Fore Street. It was intended to provide a social centre in a particularly poor neighbourhood which badly needed the nursing and other services which came to be based there.

143. Child welfare was one of the services administered from the Social Settlement. These participants in a baby show held at the Town Hall in 1913, all twins, seem by their appearance to be less in need of such services than many in the town.

144. The original Social Settlement premises at the east end of Fore Street were eventually replaced by the specially designed building seen here in a picture dated 1905.

145. Formed in 1826, the Ipswich Shipwrecked Seamen's Society was an early attempt to provide a mutual benefit fund that would take care of those left destitute as a result of shipwreck; as the legend on the society's banner proclaimed, 'Here the Widows and Orphans find a friend'. In this photograph members of the society are taking part in the Lifeboat Saturday procession in 1907.

146. The East Suffolk Hospital was founded in 1835 on Anglesea Road, the original building seen here costing a mere £2,500 when it was opened the following year. Many extensions were made over the years, almost all of which have been demolished now that a new Ipswich Hospital has been built in Heath Road.

147. Nurses and patients in a women's ward prepare to celebrate Christmas in pre-N.H.S. days.

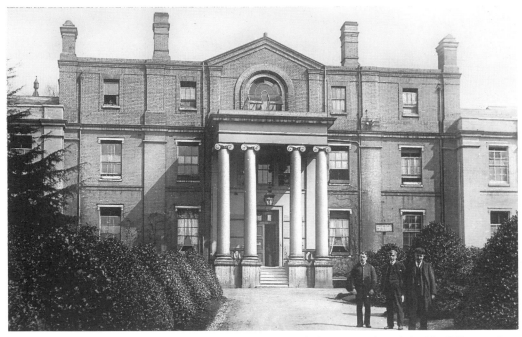

148. In 1869 the hospital was enlarged by adding a third storey to the original building, and a children's wing was added in 1875.

149. The foundations of the Welfare State were laid in the early years of this century with the passing of the National Insurance Act. The birth of the first baby to qualify his parents for maternity benefit was celebrated on 14 January 1913 by the father's fellow-workers at Turner's St Peter's Ironworks.

150. Many people did find time for sport and recreation i spite of long working hours and short holidays. In 1913 a swimming race was held between the West End Bathin Place on the Gipping and the Stoke Bathing Place downriver A film was made of the event, from which this still of the finis has been taken.

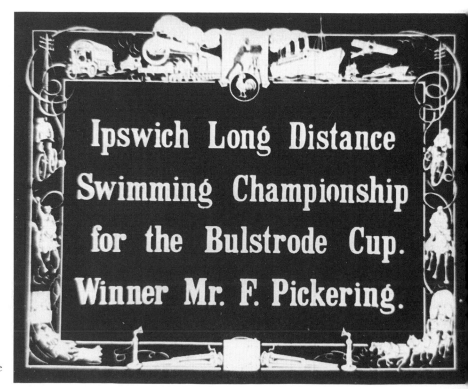

Ipswich Long Distance Swimming Championship for the Bulstrode Cup. Winner Mr. F. Pickering.

151. The title sequence of the film.

152. Many girls went 'into service' as soon as they left school, and local newspapers contained many advertisements for servants to work in middle-class houses in the town. This advertising postcard was issued by the *East Anglian Daily Times*.

153. The Ipswich Poor Children's Outing was first organised by the Ipswich and District Motorcycle Club in 1923, when about 400 children were entertained. In 1929, when no fewer than 2,400 youngsters were taken to Glemham Hall, a film was made for showing in one of the town's cinemas; this is a still from the film.

TWENTIETH-CENTURY CHANGES

154. At the turn of the century these buildings on the corner of St Nicholas Street and Falcon Street were awaiting demolition. Along with many similar properties, they were to make way for new shops considered more in keeping with the new century.

155. The coming of the electric tram necessitated not only the construction of an electricity generating station in Constantine Road and of the adjacent tram depot but the laying of more than 10 miles of new 3 ft. 6 in. gauge track. Here the new track is being laid on Cornhill in 1903.

156.   Tramcar No. 21 waits to start from the Felixstowe Road terminus outside the *Royal Oak* on the corner of Derby Road.

IPSWICH, TOP OF PRINCES STREET

157. A lively scene at the top of Princes Street about 1910, with tramcar No. 32 making for the Cornhill at the end of its journey from the station. A notice at the entrance to the Corn Exchange declares that the provision market is open.

158. A laden coal cart makes its way up Bishop's Hill as tramcar No. 15 rattles down the single track. The barber's pole on the left marks Ernest Abbott's hairdressing establishment, and on the right on the Myrtle Road corner is George Cox's butcher's shop bearing the legend 'Shipping Supplied'.

159. Tramcar No. 10 passing the junction of Wellington Street as it makes its way down Norwich Road towards the Cornhill; from there it will run on to Derby Road station.

160. In the 1930s the buildings on the east side of Cornhill occupied by the Essex & Suffolk Equitable Insurance Society came down to make way for new premises for the National Provincial Bank.

161. One of the first Railless trolleybuses introduced in 1923 arrives from the station as a tram trundles down Tavern Street. The South African War memorial was subsequently moved to Christchurch Park.

162. Timber-framed houses in Stoke Street are cleared away in 1933.

163. These old houses in Bridge Street were demolished in 1926 when Stoke Bridge was replaced. In the background is Eastern Union Mills, later to become the yeast factory of British Fermentation Products.

64. Tudor buildings on St Margaret's Plain before road widening in 1931.

65. The same buildings after the section in Margaret's Street had been demolished to allow the road to be widened.

166. New designs, new houses. An aerial view of the council housing estate laid out on what had been the town's racecourse; Nacton Road is on the extreme right.

167. New detached houses being built in the 1930s on the outskirts of the town.

168. Princess Mary was greeted by the Girl Guides when she formally opened Chantry Park, which had been given to the town by Sir Arthur Churchman, during her first visit on 20 October 1928. The Chantry had its origin in the licence granted to Edmund Daundy in 1509 to found and endow a chantry in St Lawrence's Church.

169. The First Battalion of the Suffolk Regiment marches on to the Cornhill on 17 August 1927, to be welcomed by the Mayor and members of the Corporation. The battalion had been on foreign service for no less than 17 years and was making its first recruiting march through its own county.

170. Members of the Ipswich and District Motorcycle Club pose for their photograph outside the *Running Buck* on St Margaret's Plain one Sunday morning about 1930.

171. The Ipswich and District Motorcycle Club held speed trials on the drive at Shrubland Park on 12 May 1928 to raise funds for the Ipswich and East Suffolk Hospital. This is how they advertised the event.

172. Both cars and motorcycles took part in the trials, being timed electrically over the quarter-mile course.

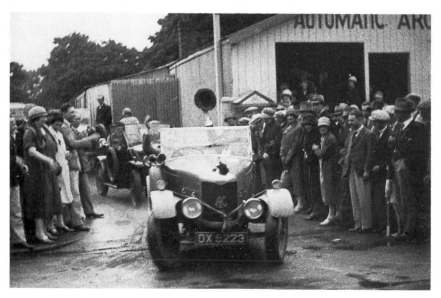

173. Events like car rallies attract large crowds of spectators in the 192 when the Ipswich and District Motorcycle Club was very active. T letters DX were an Ipswich registration.

174. Poole's Picture Palace opened in what had been the lecture hall of the Ipswich Institute on 9 March 1909. It was the town's first cinema, but was quite soon followed by others.

175. The end wall of this building in Tacket Street, bared by demolition of the adjoining property, became a hoarding advertising a show at the Hippodrome, built as a theatre in 1905.

176. The Hippodrome, founded by E. H. Bostock, decorated for the visit of Princess Mary in 1928. It later became a cinema for a period before re-opening as a revue theatre in 1941.

177. The Lyceum Theatre in Carr Street in the 1920s when it was also showing films. Its 1,100-seat auditorium was a confection of yellow and gold, liberally sprinkled with Shakespearian texts.

178. The corner of the Buttermarket and Upper Brook Street before it was widened in the 1930s. This is J. A. Symonds' chemist's shop.

179. There were also changes at the corner of Tacket Street, where the old building on the junction came down to allow the road to be widened. Alexander the Great Clothier, however, remained in Upper Brook Street for another 40 years; Henry Charles Alexander had been at No. 53 back in the 1890s.

180. Symonds Cash Chemist after the 1930s' rebuilding which took the building line back several feet to match the line to the south of the Buttermarket.

181. The Suffolk and Eastern Counties Aeroplane Club began operations at an airfield between Ipswich and Hadleigh in 1927, and the following Easter more than 5,000 people attended an air display there.

182. During the display one of the club's pilots, Miss Sylvia Edwards, arrived on the field in a car towing behind it one of the club's Blackburn Bluebirds with its wings folded. She unfolded the wings and flew off to give a demonstration.

183. The Suffolk and Eastern Counties Aeroplane Club took over the management of Ipswich Airport when it opened in 1930. To open the airport the Prince of Wales, later King Edward VIII and the Duke of Windsor, arrived there in his own Westland Wapiti for a visit to the town on 26 June 1930.

184. During his visit, the Prince carried out a number of public engagements. Here he is seen at the Arboretum with the town's first Labour mayor, Mr. A. L. Clouting.

185. A group of Ipswich firemen with one of the first motor fire engines acquired by the Ipswich fire brigade in the 1920s. Horses were used until 1920 to draw the engines to the scene of a fire.

186. The greater part of the premises of Wrinch & Sons Ltd., manufacturers of garden seats and chairs in Portman Road, were destroyed on the evening of 7 July 1928. Nearly 200 workers were thrown out of employment by the fire, which was the more unfortunate as the Labour Exchange next door was also badly burnt.

187. The blaze which destroyed the Central Cinema and other premises in Princes Street in February 1950. The fire engine standing outside the cinema is one of the Second World War tenders fitted with a trailer pump.

88. St Matthew's Street in March 1959, with a trolleybus on its way out of town. The St Matthew's roundabout at the top of Civic Drive now occupies much of the site of this picture.

89. Trolleybus No. 41, one of a batch of single-deckers built by Ransomes in 1928, seen in Princes Street in August 1953. It was withdrawn later that year.

190. Concept and reality: the dull concrete face of Greyfriars, built in the 1960s as a speculative development when it was thought Ipswich needed improved shopping facilities.

191. Concept and reality: the bright, clean face of Greyfriars as displayed by a model prepared by the developers and superimposed on an aerial photograph of the area between Wolsey Street (left) and Princes Street (right).

THE STORE OF EAST ANGLIA

FOOTMANS

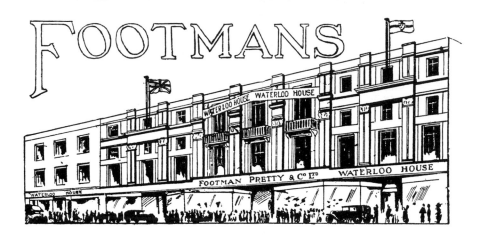

THE SHOPPING
CENTRE OF ...
IPSWICH
WITH OVER A
CENTURY'S ....
REPUTATION FOR
SERVICE & VALUE

WATERLOO
HOUSE,

FOOTMAN, PRETTY & CO., LTD.

IPSWICH

'PHONE **3737**.